Do You
KNOW
WHAT TURNS
HIM
ON?

Pat Robinson

ebooks

Published by Sourcebooks, Inc.
P.O. Box 4410, Naperville, Illinois 60567-4410
(630) 961-3900
Fax: (630) 961-2168
www.sourcebooks.com

Library of Congress Cataloging-in-Publication Data is on file with the publisher.

Printed and bound in the United States of America.

SP 10 9 8 7 6 5 4 3 2 1

Whether the two of you are a new couple or have been attached for years—or even decades—there's a lot you don't know about him when it comes to the bedroom. However open your relationship, however talkative you both may be, not everything comes to the surface naturally. It's not that someone is necessarily hiding anything. It's just that each of us is made up of so many bits of personal history, preferences, and opinions, that getting them all out there requires a lot of effort and time.

Or this book.

Do your best to answer the one hundred questions in this little test and have him check your answers.

At its best, the exercise can help you to mesh better as a twosome—it'll improve your couple fitness. At the very least, if you go in with the right attitude, you'll both have some fun. And it'll get you talking.

Count ten points for each correct answer:

Above 900: Congratulations. If you score this high, you must be sizzlin'.

800–900: A solid performance. You're doing something right.

600–790: Not bad, but try for a little more openness in bed.

Below 600: Some effort will help. Go back over your answers and pay attention. You can have a lot of fun learning.

Good luck.
—*P. R.*

do **YOU** know?

1. **ON A LONG WEEKEND TOGETHER, WOULD HE BE MORE TURNED ON BY:**
   .... Being awakened for a love session in the middle of the night?
   .... Making love first thing in the morning?

2. **WHERE DOES HE *REALLY* LIKE TO BE KISSED?**
   .... Lips
   .... Ears
   .... Palms
   .... Back of the neck
   .... Sides
   .... Feet

3. WHICH SCENE WOULD BE HIS CHOICE FOR AN OUTDOOR ROMP?

.... On the lawn, on your softest blanket

.... In the woods, in a sleeping bag

.... In a secluded corner of a beach, on the sand

4. HE WOULD BE MORE EXCITED TO:

.... Give you a lap dance

.... Receive a lap dance from you

5. WHEN YOU TALK ABOUT AN OLD FLAME, HE:

.... Feels insanely jealous that anyone else ever had you

.... Feels really terrific "because now you're mine"

.... Honestly does not care one way or the other

6. **DOES HE HAVE A FAVORITE MEMORY OF ONE SPECIAL TIME YOU'VE SPENT TOGETHER, IN BED OR OTHERWISE? WHICH?**

....

....

7. **WHAT DOES HE THINK ABOUT QUICKIES?**

.... They can be really, really hot.

.... Why bother?

8. **AFTER SEX, HE PREFERS TO FALL ASLEEP:**

.... In the spoons position

.... Snuggled head-to-chest

.... Close, but not touching

9. **WHEN YOU SLEEP IN THE SPOONS POSITION HE WOULD RATHER BE:**

.... Big spoon

.... Little spoon

do **YOU** know?

10. HE WAS A VIRGIN UNTIL AGE:

....

....

11. HE WOULD RATHER WATCH A HARDCORE FILM:
.... With you
.... With a group of friends
.... Alone
.... Never

**12. THE BEST WAY TO PRESS HIS PLEASURE
       BUTTON IS:**

....

....

....

13. **IF YOU CALLED HIM AND WHISPERED SOMETHING STEAMY, YOU WOULD EXPECT TO HEAR:**

   .... An equally steamy response

   .... "I'm busy. What do you want?"

   .... "Who is this?"

14. **IN HOW MANY LANGUAGES CAN HE WHISPER "I LOVE YOU"?**

   ....

   ....

15. **IF YOU AND HE STRIPPED AND JUST GAZED INTO EACH OTHER'S EYES WITHOUT TOUCHING, WHO WOULD LAST LONGEST?**

   ....

   ....

16. SEX WITH A STRANGER? HE WOULD SAY:

.... "If the stranger is hot, I might."

.... "Let me think about it."

.... "No way, José!"

17. HOW ABOUT *YOU* HAVING SEX WITH A STRANGER? HE WOULD SAY:

.... "If the stranger is hot, I might not object."

.... "Let me think about it."

.... "No way, José!"

18. A BIG MIRROR ON THE CEILING OVER THE BED? TO HIM, IT'S:

.... A turn-on

.... Tacky, tacky

.... Just something else to have to keep clean

19. WHICH OF THESE WOULD MAKE HIS TEMPERATURE RISE?

.... A super-long kiss with only lips touching

.... Washing each other's hair while you shower together

.... Doing it in a public place where you might get caught

.... Not wearing any underwear

20. WHICH OF THESE DOES HE THINK IS THE BEST MUSIC TO PLAY TO GET SOME ACTION IN THE BEDROOM?

.... Micheal Bublé

.... Barry White

.... Justin Timberlake

.... Ravel's *Boléro*

21. **WHICH WOULD HE CHOOSE TO SET THE MOOD?**
.... Two glasses of cold champagne
.... A six-pack of beer
.... A pot of super-strong coffee

22. **DANCING A LONG, SLOW DANCE AT HOME, WITHOUT MUSIC, IS SOMETHING HE:**
.... Might easily suggest
.... Would gladly do if you started it
.... Could never get into

23. **TO HIM, THE IDEA OF LICKING WARM, MELTED CHOCOLATE AND WHIPPED CREAM OFF THE BEST PARTS OF EACH OTHER'S BODIES IS:**
.... Sexy
.... Silly

24. AND BREAKFAST IN BED IS:
.... Romantic
.... Sappy

25. A BIG BOUQUET FOR NO SPECIAL OCCASION?
.... Sweet
.... A waste

26. TIPPING THE PIANO PLAYER TO PLAY A FAVORITE SONG?
.... Charming
.... Foolish

27. AND PROPOSING ON BENDED KNEE IS:
.... Tender
.... Stupid

do **YOU** know?

28. **YOU'RE IN BED, HALF WATCHING TV, HALF FOOLING AROUND. THINGS START TO GET SERIOUS JUST AS THE NEWS COMES ON. WHAT DOES HE DO?**

.... Leaves the news on

.... Changes to something lighter

.... Turns the TV off

.... Asks "Do you want it on or off?"

29. **WHAT'S THE HIGHEST NUMBER OF ORGASMS HE HAS EXPERIENCED IN A SINGLE TWENTY-FOUR-HOUR PERIOD?**

.... One

.... Two or three

.... Four or five

.... More than five

30. DOES HE HAVE ANY SEX TOYS?

.... Of course not!

.... I don't know, and I don't want
to know.

.... I don't know, but I'd love to find out.

.... Sure, a ....

**31. HE WOULD RATHER LOOK AT YOU
WEARING:**

.... Something see-through

.... Something tight in the right places

.... Nothing at all

32. HE WOULD GO SKINNY-DIPPING:

.... In a private pool

.... At a secluded beach, with no
one around

.... At an openly nude beach with
a crowd

.... Nowhere, never, no how

33. COULD HE LIE BACK AND LET YOU ADMINISTER A MASSAGE ALL OVER HIS BODY WITHOUT GETTING WORKED UP?

.... Sure

.... Maybe sometimes

.... Not a chance

34. WOULD HE AGREE TO MAKE A VIDEO OF ONE OF YOUR LOVE SESSIONS?

.... Yes, eagerly

.... Reluctantly, perhaps

.... No, no, no

35. CAN HE GET AROUSED AS READILY WHEN FULLY CLOTHED AS WHEN NAKED?

.... Absolutely

.... Maybe

.... Unlikely

do
YOU
know?

36. IF YOU SUGGESTED A GAME OF STRIP POKER, WHAT WOULD HE SAY?

.... "Uh…not right now."

.... "Red cards and black cards are wild!"

37. DOES HE THINK CERTAIN FOODS ARE APHRODISIACS? WHICH?

....

....

....

38. IN THE BEDROOM, HE PREFERS:

.... Lights on

.... Lights off

39. HIS CHOICE DURING THE MOST INTIMATE MOMENTS:

.... Eyes open

.... Eyes closed

40. IF THE TWO OF YOU CHECKED IN TO A MOTEL NEAR HOME IN THE MIDDLE OF THE DAY, AND MADE LOVE UNTIL YOU WERE EXHAUSTED, HE WOULD FEEL:

.... Slightly slimy

.... Really guilty

.... Terrific

41. HOW DOES HE FEEL ABOUT TRYING A NEW POSITION?

.... He's always up for trying something new

.... He'll experiment, but always goes back to the tried and true

.... He sticks with the familiar

42. WHERE *WOULDN'T* HE MAKE OUT?

.... In the rain

.... On the grass

.... In a movie theater

.... Behind a church

43. IF YOU SAID, "THE MOST POWERFUL SEX ORGAN IS THE BRAIN," HE WOULD:

.... Agree

.... Disagree

44. DOES HE REMEMBER YOUR FIRST MEETING?

.... Yes

.... No

45. HOW ABOUT YOUR FIRST KISS?

.... Yes

.... No

do **YOU** know?

46. THE FIRST TIME YOU MADE LOVE?
.... Yes
.... No

47. WHAT MOVIE MAKES HIM HORNY?

....

....

....

48. IF YOU COULD ONLY HAVE FIVE MINUTES OF EITHER HUGGING OR KISSING, WHICH WOULD HE CHOOSE?
.... Hugging
.... Kissing

49. **"SEX IS ALWAYS BETTER WITH A LITTLE ALCOHOL OR POT." HE WOULD SAY THIS STATEMENT IS:**

.... True

.... False

.... Not even worth considering

50. **HE THINKS SMOKING CIGARETTES IS:**

.... Sexy

.... A turn-off

.... No big deal

51. **WHERE IS HE TICKLISH? HOW TICKLISH?**

	a little	very	not at all
Neck			
Armpits			
Stomach			
Groin			
Feet			

52. HAS HE EVER GOOGLED AN EX'S NAME OR PURPOSELY DRIVEN OR WALKED BY AN EX'S HOME?

.... Yes, within the past year

.... Yes, a year or more ago

.... Never

53. IF HE GOT A TATTOO—FOR THE FIRST TIME OR A NEW ONE—WHAT WOULD IT DEPICT?

....

....

54. WHAT DOES HE THINK ABOUT BODY PIERCING?

....

....

55. DOES HE HAVE ANY SCARS? WHERE?

....

....

do **YOU** know?

56. WOULD HE CONSIDER CHANGING HIS HAIR COLOR?

.... Yes, seriously

.... He'd at least toy with the idea

.... Uh-uh

57. HOW ABOUT PLASTIC SURGERY?

.... Yes, seriously: a .... job

.... He'd at least toy with the idea

.... Uh-uh

58. BEING COMPLETELY ALONE FOR FORTY-EIGHT HOURS WOULD MAKE HIM:

.... Super-relaxed

.... A little itchy for company

.... Very unhappy

59. "I'VE SEEN PAINTINGS IN MUSEUMS THAT ARE SO SENSUOUS THEY TURN ME ON." HE WOULD:

.... Agree

.... Disagree

60. WHAT FAMOUS PERSON DOES HE THINK YOU LOOK LIKE?

....

....

....

61. IS THERE A CELEBRITY HE WOULD LIKE TO GET BETWEEN THE SHEETS WITH (EVEN IN A FANTASY)? WHO?

....

....

....

62. FOR MATTRESS TALK, HE PREFERS:

.... Trading sweet nothings

.... Real professions of love

.... Instruction and guidance

.... A little dirty talk

.... Silence

63. WHAT DOES HE THINK ABOUT SEX IN A CAR?

.... "It's for teenagers."

.... "Hey, if the mood strikes, why not?"

.... "Super idea!"

64. "LET'S WATCH A ROMANTIC MOVIE IN BED AND KISS WHENEVER THERE'S A KISS ON-SCREEN." CAN YOU IMAGINE HIM SUGGESTING THAT GAME?

.... Sure

.... It's possible

.... Not a chance

65. FIRESIDE ROMANCE? HE WOULD:

.... Really get into it

.... Go along

.... Worry about stray sparks

66. "LET'S GIVE EACH OTHER 100 KISSES ALL OVER THE FACE AND NECK, BUT SAVE THE LIPS FOR LAST." WOULD HE EVER PLAY THAT GAME?

.... Yes, but he'd never last to 100

.... Yes, all the way

.... Not that one

67. HOW LONG COULD THE TWO OF YOU JUST HUG?

.... Less than ten seconds

.... Ten seconds to a minute

.... More than a minute

68. HOW LONG COULD THE TWO OF YOU SIT AND HOLD HANDS BEFORE HE'D ESCALATE THE ACTIVITY?

.... Less than ten seconds

.... Ten seconds to a minute

.... More than a minute

69. COULD YOU TAKE A BATH TOGETHER WITHOUT HIM WANTING TO DO SOMETHING OTHER THAN GET CLEAN?

.... Definitely

.... Could be

.... Are you kidding?

70. SEX STANDING UP IS SOMETHING HE THINKS IS:

.... Appealing

.... More trouble than it's worth

.... Distasteful

71. **"I'D LOVE TO LOOK AT EROTIC PICTURES IN A MAGAZINE WITH YOU." HE WOULD:**

.... Never say that

.... Agree if you said it

.... Say it and whip out a magazine

72. **WITH ABSOLUTELY NOBODY CLOSE ENOUGH TO SEE, WOULD HE TAKE PLEASURE IN WALKING COMPLETELY NAKED:**

.... Around the house?

.... Around the yard?

.... Around the block?

73. **WHICH SEASONAL AMOROUS ACTIVITY WOULD MAKE HIM HAPPIER?**

.... Snuggling under a blanket on a chilly winter morning

.... Lounging on top of the sheets on a warm summer night

do **YOU** know?

74. **HE THINKS THAT FAKING AN ORGASM IS:**
.... Never acceptable
.... Sometimes a helpful part of lovemaking
.... Very common, very harmless

75. **OF THE PLACES OUTSIDE THE BEDROOM WHERE THE TWO OF YOU HAVE GOTTEN IT ON, WHAT'S HIS FAVORITE?**

....

....

76. **"I EXPECT TO CONTINUE TO ENJOY SEX TWENTY OR THIRTY YEARS FROM NOW." HE WILL:**
.... Agree
.... Disagree

77. WHICH STATEMENT WOULD HE AGREE WITH?

.... "Writing love letters is a sweet thing to do."

.... "Putting intimate thoughts on paper is dangerous."

78. DO YOU HAVE AN ARTICLE OR OF CLOTHING THAT HE FINDS ESPECIALLY TEMPTING?

.... Yes: ....

.... Nothing special

79. WHAT DOES HE THINK OF AS "OUR SONG"?

....

....

....

80. STROKING EACH OTHER UNDER THE TABLE AT A RESTAURANT—HE WOULD CALL THAT:

.... A no-no

.... A yes-yes

81. WHAT'S HIS GENERAL VIEW OF PDA—A PUBLIC DISPLAY OF AFFECTION?

.... "If you're not poking anyone's eye out, it's your business."

.... "It depends on how public and how much affection."

.... "Hey, get a room!"

82. HAS HE WATCHED ANOTHER COUPLE GO ALL THE WAY?

.... Yes, but the details are fuzzy.

.... Yes—would you like to hear all about it?

.... Sorry, never had a show like that.

do **YOU** know?

83. IF SOMEONE OFFERED YOU A MILLION DOLLARS FOR A ROLL IN THE HAY, HE WOULD:

.... Tell you to take the deal

.... Advise you to negotiate for a better price

.... Suggest that you think it over carefully

.... Stand there speechless

.... Scream in horror

84. HE ENJOYS LOOKING IN THE MIRROR IN THE NUDE:

.... From the neck up

.... From the waist up

.... From the waist down

.... Full body

.... Only in the dark

85. **WOULD HE RATHER BE:**
.... Slowly undressed, piece by piece?
.... Gently slathered from north to south with warm oil?
.... Completely covered with juicy, ripe berries, ready to be nibbled?
.... All three: undressed, slathered, and covered?

86. **WOULD HE CONSIDER GETTING INTO BED WEARING A HAT?**
.... Yes, no reason not to
.... Yes, but laughing all the way
.... Can't even imagine it

87. IN THE EVENT OF A FIRE, WHAT GIFT FROM YOU WOULD HE SAVE FIRST?

....

....

88. COULD HE TELL THE LEFT PART OF YOUR CHEST FROM THE RIGHT WHILE BLINDFOLDED?

.... No problem

.... Problem

89. WOULD HE PREFER YOU TO USE YOUR LIGHTEST TOUCH:

.... Working from the face and neck all the way down, s-l-o-w-l-y?

.... Right at the target, over and over until you can't take it anymore?

90. **IF YOU BOTH GET COMPLETELY STICKY AND SWEATY DURING STEAMY SEX, HE THINKS THAT IT:**

.... Puts a damper on the whole thing

.... Makes the action even better

.... Makes no difference either way

91. **IF SOMEONE IS IN THE ROOM NEXT TO YOU WHEN YOU'RE BUSY EXCITING EACH OTHER, THAT MAKES HIM:**

.... More passionate

.... Less passionate

.... Just the same

92. **HE WOULD RATHER STUDY A SEX MANUAL:**

   .... With you, to put the tips to immediate use

   .... Alone, to apply later

93. **HE THINKS PASSING FOOD MOUTH-TO-MOUTH WHILE KISSING IS:**

   .... Exciting

   .... Disgusting

   .... A good way to cut calories by sharing

94. **LOCKING EYES AT JUST THE RIGHT MOMENT MAKES HIM FEEL:**

   .... Close to you

   .... Uncomfortable

95. WHEN IT COMES TO BAWDY JOKES, HE:

.... Loves to hear 'em, loves to tell 'em

.... Will gladly listen, but can never tell
them right

.... Doesn't really enjoy them

96. WHEN CHOOSING SIDES IN A LARGE BED, HE PREFERS:

.... The left

.... The right

.... The side closer to the window

.... The side closer to the door

.... The side closer to the radio, clock,
or phone

.... The side closer to the bathroom

97. HE THINKS GIVING PET NAMES TO BODY PARTS IS:

.... Childish

.... Fun

do **YOU** know?

98. HIS HAIR PART IS:

.... On the left

.... On the right

.... In the center

99. FOR A GETAWAY WITH YOU, PRICE NO OBJECT, WHICH WOULD HE PREFER?

.... A weekend at a luxury resort with a heart-shaped tub

.... A full week at a simple, private cottage in the woods

100. "LOVE AT FIRST SIGHT IS A NICE IDEA, BUT THERE'S REALLY NO SUCH THING." HE BELIEVES:

.... "Unfortunately, that's right."

.... "Yes, love at first sight is possible."